40 NEW TESTAMENT
BIBLE STORIES

ANDY ROBB

CONTENTS

EEK, WE'RE GREEK!

We catch up with the Jewish people (the Israelites) a few hundred years before Jesus was born – 329 years to be precise. Because the Israelites had, for the most part, turned their backs on God, they'd lost His hand of protection.

So when Alexander the Great came along looking for nations to conquer, Israel was a sitting duck.

Up till this point, the Greeks had not really done much conquering. It was Alexander's dad, Philip of Macedon, who united Greece and began to take them to war. Philip was a mighty warrior who dreamed of ruling over a vast empire. First off, he booted out the Persians who'd invaded his country and then set about doing some invading of his own. Just when

it looked like his dreams might come true, Philip died and his teenage son Alexander took over.

Alexander may have been a mighty warrior like his dad (he was a very tall and imposing guy) but he was also well educated and had a famous philosopher called Aristotle as his private tutor.

It might sound a bit big-headed to call himself Alexander the Great but he actually really was a great leader. During his short life, he conquered many countries and created a gigantic Greek empire.

When Alexander rocked up at Israel's borders, the Jewish people had no choice but to put out the welcome mat for him. It was that or be destroyed. In return for carrying on with their religious practices, the Jews paid taxes to the Greeks. They also gradually took on the Greek language. Not only did this help them understand their new masters, but certain Jews would one day be able to tell people from all over the Greek empire the good news about Jesus.

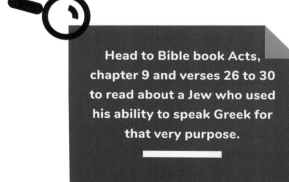

Head to Bible book Acts, chapter 9 and verses 26 to 30 to read about a Jew who used his ability to speak Greek for that very purpose.

ODD GODS!

A few hundred years before Jesus was born, it was the Greeks who dominated much of the known world and their empire stretched far and wide. Then, rather suddenly, their leader (Alexander the Great) died. In his short life of just 33 years, he had achieved much but now it was for others to rule the empire he'd created, which included the newly-conquered land of Israel.

The Greeks didn't worship the God of the Jews. In fact, they preferred to worship all manner of gods (and goddesses) depending on their mood.

For instance, Nike (yes, like the brand of trainers) was thought of as the goddess of victory, so she was very popular with soldiers going into battle.

There was also Zeus who they believed carried a thunderbolt around and hurled it at his enemies.

And not forgetting Poseidon who the Greeks gave credit to for destroying cities and causing earthquakes.

For a while the Greeks tolerated the Jewish religious practices, but when another leader came to power all that changed. Epiphanes (as he chose to be called) began to make life difficult for the Jews. Not only did he outlaw their religious way of life, but he decreed that they must worship Zeus.

He added insult to injury by sacrificing a pig to Zeus on the altar in Jerusalem's temple.

As far as the Jews were concerned the Greeks had gone too far. A Jewish priest (Mattathias) and his five sons raised an army of rebels and began a war against their Greek oppressors, which lasted many years. After Mattathias died, his son, Judas Maccabeus, took over as their leader and successfully took back the temple for the Jews.

To find out why the Jews mistakenly thought that Jesus would free them from tyranny head to Bible book Zechariah, chapter 9 and verse 9.

ROAMING ON ROMAN ROADS!

The nation of Israel was finally enjoying a period of freedom having managed to take back control of their land after being ruled by the Greeks. OK, so they'd not managed to shake off some of the Greek influences such as their language, but they were able to get back to doing lots of things the Jewish way, including their worship of God.

That said, it wasn't all plain sailing. They still needed a leader but who would that be? There were a lot of power-hungry people who wanted the job, and it caused no end of squabbling. Things eventually came to a head when a couple of brothers called Hyrcanus and Aristobolus both wanted to be king. There was only one crown so someone had to choose between them. So, they hit upon the idea of asking Rome to mediate.

For your info, the Roman empire was enjoying a bit of a growth spurt at that particular time and were always looking for new lands to conquer. The invitation from Israel seemed too good a chance to pass up, and in the year 63 BC the Roman general Pompey moved in along with his massive army.

That wasn't quite what the Jews were expecting but it was too late. Having booted out the Greeks, the Jews now found themselves under the thumb of the Romans.

In a bid to keep the Jews on their side, the Romans installed Jewish rulers of their choosing to govern things on their behalf.

One of the benefits of the Romans invading their land is that they were excellent road builders and they built roads all over their empire to make transportation safe and easy. That's where the saying 'all roads lead to Rome' comes from.

But God had other ideas for these ancient motorways. When the time was right to send the Christ (a special person sent by God) to Israel, His message would spread so much quicker by these roads!

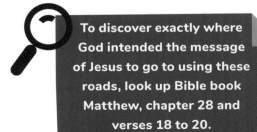

To discover exactly where God intended the message of Jesus to go to using these roads, look up Bible book Matthew, chapter 28 and verses 18 to 20.

CRACKERS CHRISTMAS

Christmas is one of my favourite times of the year. Christmas carols, roast turkey, presents under the tree – I love it all. But rewind a couple of thousand years to a place called Bethlehem and you'd soon find out that if you happened to mention Christmas, no one would have had a clue what you were talking about. Being a clever clogs, you've probably worked out why. It's because Jesus hadn't been born yet and without Jesus there isn't any Christmas.

To get you up to speed on what's been happening, Mary and Joseph (Jesus' parents) had travelled to Bethlehem and, as we catch up with them, Jesus has just been born. Jesus wasn't any old baby, He was God's one and only Son. What's even more amazing is that nobody in Bethlehem had the foggiest idea who'd been born right under their noses. But that was all about to change.

Crazy as it seems, the first people that God let in on His big secret were a bunch of bog-standard shepherds. Nothing personal, fellas, I'm just saying it how it is. This was probably looking like it was going to be just another ordinary and uneventful night out on the hills around Bethlehem when, without a word of warning – BAM! – an angel appeared. Wow, that certainly got their attention!

The shepherds were scared silly. Once the angel had calmed them down, he announced the good news that a baby had been born in the nearby town and, even better, this baby was going to be the rescuer of the world. He then suggested that they go and pay this special baby a visit.

As if the shepherds hadn't had enough shocks for one night, an entire angel army then showed up, praising God and singing their hearts out to Him. What a unforgettable night it had been for those fellas!

Do you think they took the angel up on his offer? You can find the answer to that question by looking up Bible book Luke, chapter 2 and reading verses 15 through to 18.

DIVINE DUNKER

If you go to see a TV show being recorded there's often a warm-up person who comes on beforehand to get the audience in a good mood. When it comes to the Bible, John the Baptist was Jesus' warm-up man. Not that he set out to put people in a good mood, but get them ready he most certainly did. John was a close relative of Jesus and he had been born just a few months ahead of Him. The star of this Bible story had been lined up from the word go to announce to the world that Jesus was on His way. That was going to be his life's work and John took his job seriously.

We catch up with John in the Judean desert wearing a rather uncomfortable camel-hair tunic held together by a natty belt around his waist. As if that wasn't barmy enough you should hear about his diet. Locusts and wild honey! They say that a spoonful of sugar helps the medicine go down but I reckon you'd need an awful lot of honey to take away the taste of a locust. Yuckky yoo!

Although he was living out in the back of beyond, John had attracted quite a lot of interest because of what he had to say. His message was that people needed to repent (that means to turn around). Turn around from what? From leading lives that make do without God, that's what!

John was giving people the chance to turn from their wicked ways by being baptised (that's how he got his nickname of 'Baptist') in the nearby River Jordan. Being baptised simply means getting dunked in water to represent all the grot in your life being washed away by God.

One day, who should show up but Jesus Himself? Jesus was now around 30 years old and for all of that time He hadn't stepped over the line even once. The Bible says that there was no sin (bad stuff) to be found in Jesus whatsoever. Wow! But here's the amazing thing: Jesus still wanted to be baptised by John.

It has to be said that John couldn't believe it either. Surely not! This wasn't right – Jesus should be baptising him.

> When Jesus was baptised, the Holy Spirit came down like a dove and God spoke out loud. Want to know what He said? Try looking in Bible book Matthew, chapter 3 and verse 17.

VERY TEMPTING

How would you fancy going without food for 40 days? Not much, I reckon. Well, that's precisely what Jesus did right after He'd been baptised in the River Jordan.

Filled with God's power, Jesus was getting ready to reveal Himself as God's Son. His mission was to patch things up between people and God, but first Jesus needed to be tested to make sure He was fit for the job. Jesus could only do what God required if He was perfect, which meant He couldn't so much as do one teensy thing wrong. That might sound completely impossible to you and me, but don't forget that Jesus is God. Who was going to put Jesus to the test?

None other than God's number one enemy, Satan. If Jesus succeeded in His mission to planet Earth, Satan would be defeated. The battle was on.

After 40 foodless days in the hot and sticky desert, Satan showed up. 'If you're God's Son, order these stones to turn to bread.' Satan was quoting bits of the Bible but Jesus wasn't gonna give in to God's words being twisted. Jesus immediately came back at Satan with a Bible bit of His own: 'The scripture says, "Human beings cannot live on bread alone, but need every word that God speaks."' Good move, Jesus! 1–0 to Jesus.

Satan had another go at trying to tempt Jesus away from doing what God wanted. He tried to persuade Jesus to leap off the highest part of God's Temple (in Jerusalem) and trust in God's angels to protect Him. Once again, Jesus held His ground and fired back another Bible bit to counterattack Satan's temptation. 2–0 to Jesus.

Satan had one more trick up his sleeve. He offered Jesus all the kingdoms of the world on one condition... that He worship Satan.

Did Jesus give in to Satan's tempting temptations? Check out Bible book Matthew, chapter 4 and verses 10 and 11 to find out.

NEW NICK

The nation of Israel had always been special in God's eyes. They had been handpicked by Him to show the rest of the world what He was like. It wasn't because they were better than everyone else, this was just the way God chose to do it.

Along the way, God had given the Jewish people (which was how the Israelites were also known) laws that He commanded them to live by. The religious leaders' job was to help the Jews keep these laws. When Jesus came onto the scene, many of the religious leaders of His day refused to accept that He was the Christ their scriptures had told them to expect.

But not all of the religious leaders rejected Jesus. Some of them could see that He was more than just a man, and kept an open mind on the matter. It was dangerous and unwise for these people to admit this in public, so they kept their thoughts and conversations private.

One of them was a guy called Nicodemus, who the Bible describes as a 'ruler of the Jews', so he was a top bod among the religious leaders. Nicodemus wanted to meet with Jesus and, under cover of darkness, he came to Him.

Nicodemus told Jesus he knew God had sent Him to teach them, and that He wouldn't have been able to do all the miracles He'd done if God hadn't been with Him. Jesus' reply was somewhat surprising. Rather than picking up on what Nicodemus had said, Jesus told him that the only way he could see the kingdom of God was if he was 'born again'. Nicodemus was more than a little perplexed! What on earth did Jesus mean by that?

Jesus was explaining to Nicodemus that this is also the same way someone is born into God's family. Discover how in Bible book John, chapter 3 and verses 4 through to 6.

WELL, WELL, WELL

There's an expression that talks about being in the right place at the right time. That's what happened to the woman who stars in this Bible story.

We don't know her name but we do know that she lived in a town called Sychar in Samaria. Jesus was heading back to Galilee and was passing through her neck of the woods.

It was around the middle of the day and Jesus was flaked out after walking in the heat. Time to put His feet up and rest His weary legs while His disciples popped into town to grab some lunch.

Jesus plonked Himself down by a well and waited. Meanwhile a local lady rocked up to get some water. She had absolutely no idea who Jesus was but this chance meeting (though I reckon God had set it up good and proper) with God's Son was going to change the life of this woman for good.

To the lady's surprise, Jesus asked her for a drink.

The reason it was a surprise is that Jews (and Jesus was one) made it their business not to have anything to do with Samaritans (which this lady was). But Jesus wasn't bothered with that sort of thing. He was happy to get along with anyone.

Jesus didn't miss a trick, and because they were by a well He began to talk to the woman about how He could give her living water. He said that if she drank water from the well she'd be thirsty again but if she drank the water that He was offering, she never would.

Jesus was talking about the life-giving Holy Spirit He gives to those who follow Him.

While she was still trying to get her head around what Jesus had been saying, He told her to go fetch her husband.

The woman didn't actually have a husband and she told Jesus so. He knew that! In fact He also knew that she'd had five husbands in the past. She was living with a man right now but they weren't married. Jesus told her all this and she was amazed! Only a man sent from God could know such things, so she hurried back into town to tell everyone about Jesus.

Did they believe her?

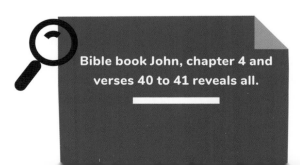

Bible book John, chapter 4 and verses 40 to 41 reveals all.

IDENTITY CRISIS

Jesus had been brought up in the town of Nazareth where He'd lived with His mum, dad, brothers and sisters. The Bible tells us that Jesus' dad made his living as a carpenter and there's every chance that Jesus joined the family business.

Other than a story about Jesus going to Jerusalem with His family when He was 12 years old, the Bible says absolutely zilch about Jesus' upbringing. The chances are that He was brought up like any normal Jewish boy. He would have been taught all about God from the Jewish Scriptures and His dad would have had a big part to play in that. Although Jesus' mum and dad (Mary and Joseph) had been told by God that their boy was going to be a special lad (well actually He was God's Son so that makes Him more than a little special I'd say), we've no idea if they blabbed about this to their family and friends or whether they just kept schtum (said nothing). That said, it's fairly safe to assume that as far as most people were concerned, Jesus was nothing out of the ordinary.

But that was all about to change. Jesus had hit the ripe old age of 30 and this was where the fun began. Jesus was on a mission to patch things up between man and God and, after 30 years of waiting in the wings, it was now time for Him to go centre stage. Having been filled with God's Holy Spirit (which was His power to do the job), Jesus sprung into action.

With a tip-top team of 12 guys to help Him, Jesus went from place to place teaching people about God and healing the sick. It didn't take long for word to get out about this miracle-working man from Nazareth. He was soon making a bit of a name for Himself and wherever Jesus went the crowds gathered.

Next stop for Jesus was His hometown. I wonder what they'd make of the carpenter's son now? Time to find out. On the Jewish Sabbath (Saturday) Jesus headed for the synagogue (where the Jews had 'church') and began to teach them what He knew about God. They were gobsmacked. Where did this guy get such wisdom from? And come to think of it, how did He do all those miracles?

Want to find out if the people of Nazareth joined Jesus' fan club?

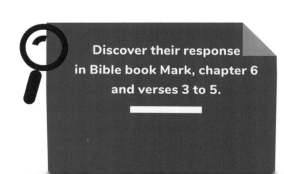

Discover their response in Bible book Mark, chapter 6 and verses 3 to 5.

A SPIT SPAT

When Jesus lived on earth, He loved demonstrating how much God cared for people by healing them. This Bible story is all about that.

Jesus and His disciples were out and about when they came across a beggar who had been blind from birth.

While the disciples had a good old ponder as to why he'd been born this way (had his parents done something wrong? Had he done something wrong?), Jesus got stuck in. As far as Jesus was concerned, if this man got healed by God's power then all those questions didn't matter. All that mattered was that God got the credit.

Anyone who'd hung around Jesus for a while would soon

have discovered that Jesus healed people in loads of different ways. There was no one formula that He worked to. And this particular day was no exception.

I suppose that Jesus could have just placed His hands on the man's eyes and healed him, but He didn't. Instead He spat on the dry ground, made some mud with the saliva, and then put it on the man's eyes. Having done this, Jesus told the man to go and wash in the Pool of Siloam.

And, guess what! The blind man was healed.

Was the blind man just fortunate that Jesus happened to have been passing by, or did God plan it all along? Who knows? One thing's for sure, his healing started a right old rumpus.

Some Jewish religious leaders heard that the chap had got his sight back and interrogated him to find out how exactly it had happened.

The thing that bugged them most seemed to be that Jesus had healed the blind man on the Jewish Sabbath. It didn't seem to make a blind bit of difference (pardon the pun) that the guy could now see. You'd think they'd be over the moon but they weren't. According to their traditions you weren't supposed to do any work (and that included healing!) on the Sabbath. If you did, it meant you were breaking the law.

So, because in their eyes Jesus had broken Jewish law, He was a sinner and they were none too pleased.

Head for Bible book John, chapter 9 and verse 16 to discover precisely what they thought of Jesus.

DOUBLE-TALKING DISCIPLE

This Bible story features a guy called Peter who was one of Jesus' 12 disciples. Peter was sometimes a bit of a hot-head but Jesus thought he was great. God makes people with different personalities and doesn't want everyone to be the same. Peter certainly wasn't the sort of guy you'd expect the Son of God (Jesus) to have on His team. Peter wasn't afraid of mouthing off or using his sword if he had to. But God always looks at people's hearts, and Peter's was sold out for Jesus so that was what mattered above everything else. Everywhere Jesus went Peter followed, hanging on His master's every word and seeing first-hand the awesome healings and miracles that Jesus did.

Nobody had ever seen the like of Jesus before but who actually was He? Was Jesus just a good man who went about doing good things? Was He perhaps a prophet of God like one of the prophets from the olden days? Or was He something else? Jesus knew full well that people were asking these sorts of questions about Him and one particular time He asked His disciples, straight up, what the word on the street was about Him. Who did people say that He was? The disciples told Jesus that some people figured He was John the Baptist and others, maybe one of the great prophets like Elijah or Jeremiah.

Then Jesus posed the same question to Peter. What was *his* take on things? Who did Peter think He was? Peter had no doubt about it. Jesus was the Christ (a special person sent by God) who would rescue the world *and* He was God's Son.

Full marks to Peter. He was spot on. Jesus told him that he'd downloaded that piece of info directly from God in heaven.

However, Peter didn't always get it right, he didn't like it when Jesus then told His disciples that He was going to be arrested and executed in Jerusalem to make all this possible. No way! Peter wasn't having that and he told Jesus so. To be fair to Peter he was only trying to protect his master but Jesus knew Satan was using Peter to try and prevent Him from accomplishing His mission on earth. What did Jesus say to Peter?

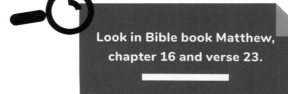

Look in Bible book Matthew, chapter 16 and verse 23.

MOUNTAIN MYSTERY

I wonder if Jesus included 'climbing mountains' in the job description when He was picking His disciples (the bunch of guys who helped Him do His stuff)? Israel had loads of mountains and hills and Jesus often climbed them to speak to the crowds below. It was much easier that way. Jesus also liked escaping to the mountains to take time out with God, and that's where we catch up with Him in this particular Bible story.

Also along for the outing were Peter, James and John, three of Jesus' best buddies. When they were completely alone, out of sight of the clamouring crowds, something weird happened to Jesus. His appearance began to change and His clothes became dazzling white. Whiter than the whitest wash from your washing machine, in fact whiter than anything you've ever seen in your life. If that wasn't enough to flabbergast the awestruck threesome, try this for size. Two famous (and long dead) guys from the Bible (Moses and Elijah) showed up. What a day this was turning out to be. Peter had ants in his pants and in his excitement and bewilderment suggested that maybe they should make three tents. One for Jesus, one for Moses and one for Elijah.

As if there weren't enough weird happenings for one day, a cloud suddenly appeared and eclipsed them with its shadow. Just when they thought that they couldn't take any more surprises, God's voice boomed out from the cloud. 'This is my own dear Son. Listen to Him!' Jesus' mates quickly looked about them but the only person they could see was Jesus. I'm guessing that the three of them couldn't wait to spill the beans and to tell all and sundry what they'd seen and heard.

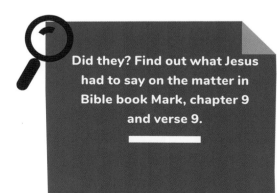

**Did they? Find out what Jesus
had to say on the matter in
Bible book Mark, chapter 9
and verse 9.**

FOLLOWER FACTS

Here's a question for you. How many disciples did Jesus have? If your answer is 12, then you are partly right. While Jesus travelled around Israel teaching people about God and healing the sick He had 12 guys as His crack team. But there were loads of other people (men and women) who also accompanied Him and who the Bible also calls disciples. So, what exactly is a disciple? In a nutshell, it's simply a person who learns from someone else. People followed Jesus so that they could learn more about God.

Jesus was never one to mince words and He spent a lot of time pointing out to the Jewish religious leaders of His day where they had got things wrong. Following God wasn't about having a reputation as some sort of holy person so that everyone would treat you like a VIP. It is an important step that requires serious thought.

One time, when Jesus had the attention of a large crowd, He decided that it was time to put the record straight on what being a disciple of His actually involved.

'If one of you is planning to build a tower, you sit down first and work out what it will cost, to see if you have enough money to finish the job. If you don't, you will not be able to finish the tower after laying the foundation; and all who see what happened will laugh at you. "This man began to build but can't finish the job!" they will say.'

Jesus was making the point that being a disciple of His wasn't always the easy option and before anyone made a decision to follow Him, it was important for them to think it through.

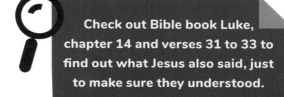

Check out Bible book Luke, chapter 14 and verses 31 to 33 to find out what Jesus also said, just to make sure they understood.

WOOLLY WANDERER

Most of us like a good story, and Jesus knew that. Rather than hit people over the head with heavy lectures about God, He used clever stories to help them understand different things about Him.

For instance, there was one time when Jesus was talking to a bunch of bad guys, and some religious leaders dropped by to listen in on what God's Son had to say. To be honest, the religious leaders hadn't exactly taken a shine to Jesus, and all this mixing with no-hopers and losers (as they saw these people) was the last straw.

Jesus decided to tell a story (the Bible calls it a parable) that would appeal to the 'no-hopers' but would really get up the noses of the religious lot. Not only that but they'd find these parables difficult to understand because their hearts were hardened towards God. Here's how it went.

A man has a 100 sheep but one of them goes and wanders off (like sheep do). What's he to do? Is it really worth all the effort of chasing off over the hillsides hunting for his missing mutton? After all, let's be honest, it was the sheep's own stupid fault for wandering off in the first place and anyway, the man would still have 99 sheep left, wouldn't he? Would anyone really miss one measly sheep?

Well, the man in Jesus' story would. He hunts high and low until he finds his woolly wanderer.

What was the point of the story? Find out in Bible book Luke, chapter 15 and verses 4 to 7.

TOMB RAIDER

I'll be straight with you. This story's not as gory as it could have been if Jesus hadn't worked wonders and done some miracle-making stuff, but let's start at the beginning.

Jesus was in Jerusalem (Israel's capital city) when news reached Him that His good buddy, Lazarus, was ill. Lazarus lived in Bethany which was only a short walk away (a couple of miles in fact). Jesus had healed oodles of people and He could have been at Lazarus' bedside in no time at all and restored His poorly pal. But that's not what Jesus did. He seemed to ignore the pleas of Mary and Martha (Lazarus' sisters) to heal their brother and stayed put in Jerusalem. What was He up to? Well, He did let slip a clue that something good was gonna come from this situation and that God would get the credit, but that didn't seem to be much help to ailing Lazarus.

Sure enough, two days later Jesus heard that Lazarus had died – and that's when He sprang into action. He headed off to Bethany with His disciples in tow. On arrival, He was met by a weeping and wailing Mary and Martha. They were distraught. They figured that if only Jesus had got there sooner then maybe their brother would still be alive. The Bible makes it clear that Jesus didn't find it easy seeing His good friends so upset, but He put His feelings on the back burner and made tracks for the tomb where the body of Lazarus had been laid. What was going on? You'll soon find out.

Jesus gave the order for the stone that covered the entrance to the tomb to be rolled away. Hang on a minute, was that a good idea? Martha pointed out to Jesus that her brother had been a gonner for four days. Surely Jesus wasn't thinking straight. Lazarus' body would be starting to rot and, being perfectly frank, it was going to smell something rotten.

Jesus reminded Martha what He'd said about God getting the credit for what was going to happen. Then the stone was rolled away. What followed next was something Martha and Mary would never forget.

To read the dramatic ending of this story, check out Bible book John, chapter 11 and verses 41 through to 44.

SHORT-CHANGED

Being a tax collector in Jesus' day meant that just about everybody hated you. Tax collectors worked for the rotten old Romans, who ruled Israel at that time and who squeezed the Jewish population for all they could get. To add insult to injury, the sneaky tax collectors bumped up the taxes by adding on a little bit extra for themselves – cheating the people out of their hard-earned dosh. Zacchaeus was one of these tax collectors, and, although he didn't know it yet, his life was about to change. Here's what happened.

Jesus had just turned up at a place called Jericho. Whenever Jesus showed up, so did the crowds. He was a celebrity and everybody wanted to see Him. Jericho was heaving with people trying to get a slice of the action – and that included

Zacchaeus. He was a short fella and wasn't going to see much if he didn't find himself a good vantage point. Just ahead of Jesus and the crowd that was following Him was a sycamore-fig tree. Zacchaeus had an idea. He raced ahead and scurried up the tree. Job done! Now he was head and shoulders above the lot of them.

As Jesus approached, Zacchaeus could see everything that was going on. Suddenly, Jesus stopped in His tracks and looked straight up at the pint-sized pilferer. Oh no! Was Jesus going to lay into him for cheating people out of their money? If He did, the crowd would probably lynch him. Jesus didn't. Of all the crazy things, Jesus called up to Zacchaeus and told him that He was coming to stay at his house. What? He couldn't be serious! Yep, He sure was. Zacchaeus clambered down the tree, overwhelmed with joy. Nobody had ever shown kindness like that to him before. Not everybody shared Zacch's elation though. People in the crowd were well-miffed that Jesus wanted to drop in at the house of a bad person like Zacchaeus. Jesus wasn't fussed what they thought. He knew full well that even a hard-nosed cheat like Zacchaeus could change for the better.

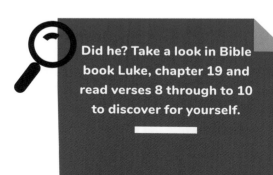

Did he? Take a look in Bible book Luke, chapter 19 and read verses 8 through to 10 to discover for yourself.

LOUD CROWD NOT ALLOWED

The clock was ticking and Jesus knew that He didn't have much time left on planet Earth. Jesus was on a mission from God and the stage was being set for His big finale in Israel's capital city, Jerusalem. Everywhere Jesus went crowds flocked to hear what He had to say and to see the miracles He did. When He showed up in Jerusalem for one last time it was the same story.

As Jesus got closer to the city, He dispatched a couple of His trusty disciples to a nearby village to fetch a colt. When the pair arrived, it was just as Jesus had told them. As they were untying the colt outside a doorway, some of the villagers asked what they were doing. When the disciples mentioned

Jesus' name, they let the pair carry on. How did Jesus know they'd find the animal there? The Bible doesn't answer that question but it does say that this very day had been predicted by one of God's prophets way back in the mists of time.

The disciples covered the colt with their cloaks and helped Jesus on to it. It didn't take much time for a large crowd to gather. People began to cover the road ahead with their cloaks and the leaves of palm trees. The crowd were treating Jesus as if He were some kind of king, but whoever heard of a king arriving at a city riding on a colt? In a horse-drawn carriage, maybe, but not the colt of a lowly donkey.

Jesus knew exactly what He was doing. Sure, He was a king, but a king of the like they'd never seen before (and never would again!). As Jesus rode into Jerusalem, people shouted out their praise to Him: 'God bless the king who comes in the name of the Lord!'

Meanwhile, the religious leaders (who by and large didn't like Jesus) were getting a bit hot under the collar. They wanted His disciples and the crowd to quit cheering Jesus.

**Want to know Jesus' sharp reply to them?
Go to Bible book Luke, chapter 19 and
verse 40 to see what it was.**

TEMPLE TURMOIL

So, Jesus arrived in Jerusalem (on a colt) and people spread palm branches on the ground, hollering 'God bless him who comes in the name of the Lord!' at the tops of their voices to welcome Him. Do you want to know what happened right after that? Well, let me tell you.

Next up, Jesus made a beeline for Jerusalem's Temple where people came to bring their sacrifices to God. The Temple was the centre of Jewish life and a mega important building for both the Jews and for God.

If Jesus was expecting the place to be shipshape and as God expected it to be then He had another think coming. Jesus was shocked by the sight that met His eyes.

Jews had to pay a Temple tax but it had to be paid with Temple currency, so the Temple had attracted cheating money changers who were charging people over the odds to change up their cash. That was a big no-no as far as Jesus was concerned. Added to which, the place was also heaving with cattle and people selling doves to be sacrificed to God.

What had happened to the peaceful and special place the Temple was supposed to be? It had been turned into little more than a market, which Jesus described as a 'hideout for thieves'. Jesus was livid that it wasn't being treated with respect. Rather than politely asking the traders to shut up shop, Jesus overturned their tables and drove out the traders.

What did Jesus say to the market traders? Check out Bible book Mark, chapter 11 and verses 16 and 17 to find out.

FINAL FEAST

The Jewish people have loads of different feasts and festivals to help remind them of stuff that God has done. The Passover Feast was one of them. It was all about remembering how God had rescued the Israelites from being slaves in Egypt.

We catch up with Jesus and His 12 disciples (His band of followers) as they celebrate the Passover in an upstairs room in the city of Jerusalem.

As they reclined around the table, Jesus dropped the bombshell that one of them was going to betray Him. What?

He must be mistaken. Nope. How would the disciples know which one of them it was? Jesus put them out of their misery and said that whoever dipped his hand into one of the bowls of food at the same time as He did was the culprit. Jesus also warned that whoever did the dirty deed to double-cross Him, was making a mega mistake and it was such a bad thing that it would be better for him if he'd never even been born.

To cut a long story short, it was Judas (their treasurer), and as soon as they'd finished eating, he legged it. Jesus knew full well that Judas was going to hand Him over to the religious leaders, who wanted His guts for garters, but He carried on with the meal regardless.

Jesus used the Passover wine and bread to tell His close buddies that He was going to allow His body to be killed and His blood to spill out as a sacrifice to God to get rid of all the grot in the world. For your info, it was the very last meal Jesus had with these guys before He died.

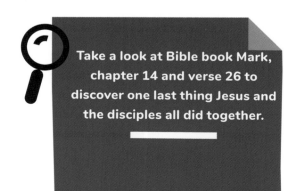

Take a look at Bible book Mark, chapter 14 and verse 26 to discover one last thing Jesus and the disciples all did together.

PRAYED – BETRAYED

You may have heard of a guy called Judas Iscariot, one of Jesus' disciples. Things started to go downhill for Judas the day a lady poured a jar of top-of-the-range perfume over Jesus to honour Him. Judas was livid. What a complete waste of money – well, at least that's what Judas thought. Who knows why he eventually gave up on Jesus, but something snapped inside him and he decided enough was enough. He simply couldn't be one of Jesus' followers any longer.

Judas was well aware that the religious leaders in Israel were chomping at the bit to get rid of Jesus. He was always challenging their way of doing things and winning hands down when it came to popularity with the crowds. They must have rubbed their hands with glee when Judas approached them with the offer of betraying Jesus into their hands.

It was a done deal. Thirty pieces of silver in exchange for Judas leading them to a secluded place to arrest Jesus, far away from all those adoring crowds. But Jesus was under no illusions where Judas' loyalties stood. During His last meal with His disciples, He had sent shock waves through the room when He predicted that one of them would betray Him.

Sure enough, that night, Jesus and the other 11 disciples were out on a hillside around Jerusalem when Judas turned up with a posse of religious leaders and an armed mob. He did the dirty deed and identified Jesus with a kiss. The religious leaders were over the moon. They finally had their man.

Throughout the night Jesus was cross-examined and then handed over to the Roman governor. Judas realised he'd made a big mistake and tried to get the religious leaders to change their minds. But they'd got what they wanted and Judas couldn't live with the horror of what he'd done.

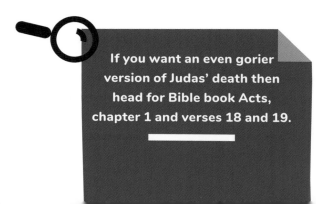

If you want an even gorier version of Judas' death then head for Bible book Acts, chapter 1 and verses 18 and 19.

PETE PANICS

Peter had spent the past three years as one of Jesus' disciples and life with Him was exciting. Everyone seemed to love Jesus – except, that is, the religious leaders who were teeth-gnashingly jealous of God's Son.

Suddenly, Peter's world had come crashing down around his ears. His master had just been arrested by those scheming religious leaders – what would happen now? One minute Jesus was teaching the adoring crowds about God and healing the sick, and the next He was on trial at the home of the Jewish high priest.

Peter was lurking in the shadows outside, trying to find out what had become of Jesus, when one of the high priest's servant girls accused him to his face of being something to do with Jesus. If you know anything about Peter you'll know that he was a confident, upfront sort of guy who'd do anything for Jesus, but not at that moment.

Peter was caught off guard and denied it, point blank. After all the time he'd spent with Jesus, he pretended that he didn't know Him. How crazy is that? You can't go around disowning your friends just to protect your own skin. But that's precisely what Peter was doing. To add insult to injury, Peter swore that he didn't know who Jesus was not once, but three times. I can only guess that he must have been so scared stiff of getting arrested himself that he'd spout out almost anything to get himself off the hook.

Sad to say, Jesus had actually warned Peter that he'd do this and that it would happen before the cockerel crowed.

Take a look at Bible book Matthew, chapter 26 and verse 75 to see how spot on Jesus had been.

SON DOWN

Every Easter, people remember the day that Jesus (God's Son) allowed Himself to be punished for all the bad stuff human beings have ever done. The thing is, however hard you try, it's just about impossible to get your head around what Jesus had to endure.

The story so far is that Jesus' enemies had got their way and made absolutely certain that Jesus had got the death sentence. They didn't like Him and the sooner He was out of the way, the better, was how they saw it.

Jesus had been well and truly stitched up (even though He was perfectly innocent) and handed over by His enemies to the Roman rulers of Israel to do their dirty work for them. Jesus was going to be executed by being nailed to a big wooden cross and then left to hang on it until He was dead.

The Roman soldiers were experts at this sort of thing and didn't need telling twice to lay into Jesus when He was handed over to them to be killed. Jesus was whipped, stripped and then had a crown made out of sharp thorns pressed onto His head to mock Him because of the claim that He was the King of the Jews. The Roman soldiers milked this for all it was worth and thought that pretending to worship Him as a king was a big joke. They beat Him, sneered at Him and spat at Him, then led Him out to the place of execution.

To add insult to injury Jesus was forced to carry His own cross through the streets of Jerusalem to Golgotha, where He met His end. Was Jesus really God's one and only Son or did the fact that He suffered a gruesome death prove that He was powerless?

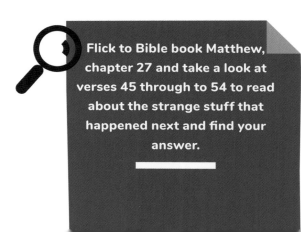

Flick to Bible book Matthew, chapter 27 and take a look at verses 45 through to 54 to read about the strange stuff that happened next and find your answer.

NOW YOU SEE HIM

The Roman rulers of Israel had executed Jesus by nailing His body to a wooden cross and leaving Him there until He died. Jesus' body was then laid to rest in a tomb. This had all happened on the Friday, but it was now Sunday.

Two of Jesus' followers (Mary and Mary Magdalene) wanted to pay their last respects to Him but they'd had to wait until the Jewish Sabbath had passed. They turned up at the tomb armed with spices to cover Jesus' dead body. Just one problem. Someone had rolled a stone in front of the entrance to the tomb. The two ladies weren't going to be able to shift that humungous rock in a month of Sundays.

The spoilsport Romans had also posted soldiers outside
the tomb just to make sure that nobody nicked Jesus' body.
Rumours had circulated that Jesus was going to come
back to life again, and if that happened it would be rather
embarrassing for the Romans.

One thing nobody had bargained on was God getting
involved. That was the last thing they needed. Tough! Being
stuck in a tomb wasn't part of the plan for God's one and only
Son. Just to prove it, God dispatched a shiny angel to scare
the pants off the Roman soldiers. It certainly did the trick! One
look at the awesome being was all it took to make them keel
over with fright. While the guards cowered in the corner, the
angel casually rolled the whopper of a stone away to reveal
the entrance to the tomb. The angel broke the news to the
two women as best he could – Jesus wasn't there anymore.
He made them take a peek inside the tomb and – guess what
– no Jesus.

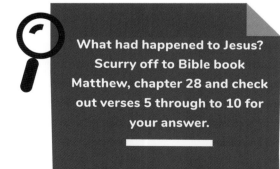

**What had happened to Jesus?
Scurry off to Bible book
Matthew, chapter 28 and check
out verses 5 through to 10 for
your answer.**

ROCKET MAN

Watching a space rocket leave the launch pad and shoot skyward at a rate of knots is a brilliant sight. But imagine seeing a human being doing something similar. It happened around the time that Jesus had been raised from the dead (brought back to life by God) after being executed on a wooden cross. At this point Jesus now had a new body that looked and felt human but could also come and go like the body of an angel. Wow!

Jesus had appeared in His heaven-and-earth-type body to hundreds of His followers over a period of 40 days after His resurrection but now, His time on earth was just about up. Jesus was packing His bags (not literally of course) and getting ready to go back to heaven where He'd originally come from.

First, though, Jesus was having a meal with His disciples (that's the bunch of guys who would carry on from Him when He'd left) and during it He gave them their final instructions.

Top of the list was that on no account were they to leave Jerusalem (where they were based) until they had been filled with God's Holy Spirit. The plan was that once Jesus had returned to heaven He'd send the Holy Spirit to take over from Him back on earth.

Everything Jesus did, He did in God's power, and it was going to be no different for His disciples. A little while back Jesus had told His team that they would do the same things that He had: miracles, healings, bringing the dead back to life. Without the power of the Holy Spirit this was going to be a complete non-starter! Only God can do that sort of stuff, and they knew it.

After telling His disciples that not only would they be power-packed witnesses in Jerusalem, but that He planned for them to go and tell the whole world about Him, Jesus did something amazing! And that was when His disciples got to see the spectacular sight I was talking about at the beginning.

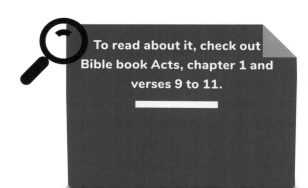

To read about it, check out Bible book Acts, chapter 1 and verses 9 to 11.

POWER SHOWER

The past three years had been a bit of a whirlwind for Jesus' disciples. Jesus had plucked them out of their humdrum lives to become His followers and to learn to do the things He did. It all came to an abrupt end when Jesus was put to death by Israel's Roman rulers.

Then, three days later, Jesus came back to life, before returning to heaven a few weeks after that. Jesus had gone and left this motley bunch of disciples in charge of carrying on His work of telling people about God and demonstrating that God loved them. But how were they going to do that? Jesus was God. They were just ordinary people. Jesus had already thought of that and had instructed them to wait in Jerusalem for something that would give them all the power they'd ever need. What was this special thing? I'll tell you. It was the Holy Spirit.

Once Jesus was back in heaven, the plan was for Him to send the Holy Spirit to live in His followers. The Holy Spirit brings God's power and life and with Him living inside them they'd be unstoppable. So, Jesus' followers were hanging out in Jerusalem, waiting for what Jesus had promised them.

Jerusalem was heaving with visitors who'd come to celebrate the Jewish festival of Pentecost. Suddenly, as if from nowhere, the whooshing noise of a mighty wind filled the room. It was God's Spirit announcing His arrival. As if that wasn't enough proof that God was in the house, something that looked like tongues of fire fell on each of their heads. Fear not! They didn't get singed scalps. This wasn't real fire, just the Holy Spirit's way of making an appearance. The Bible tells us that everyone was filled with the Holy Spirit. That meant that God was now living inside them. But God wasn't finished with this bunch of bowled-over believers. When they started to talk it wasn't their native Galilean language they spoke.

Want to know what language these Holy Spirit-filled followers began to blurt out? Take a look in Bible book Acts, chapter 2 and have a scan through verses 5 to 11.

JAMMY
JERUSALEM

There was some awesome stuff going on soon after the world's first church was started. It was in a place called Jerusalem, not long after Jesus had returned to heaven.

Before He went, Jesus handed over to His followers the job of carrying on where He'd left off. This meant telling people that Jesus had taken the punishment for all the wrong stuff they'd done – which made it possible for them to be friends with God again. As the icing on the cake, and to prove God was for real, His followers were given the power and authority to perform the same sort of miracles that Jesus did while He was on earth.

The Bible says that this was precisely what the apostles (the 12 main leaders of this first church) were up to, as we drop in on them.

Such was the impact these guys were making that the church just grew and grew. There were thousands of them, so finding a building to fit in was a non-starter. That's why they hung out in what was called Solomon's Colonnade. Although these believers in Jesus had a fantastic reputation, the people who were not part of their number kept their distance. I guess they were a bit awestruck by the amazing miracles and didn't quite know what to make of it all.

That didn't stop people becoming followers of Jesus though, and the church just kept on growing and growing.

One thing's for sure: people wanted what this power-packed church had to offer and flocked to the apostles with their sick. It didn't matter how the sick got there – be it on beds or mats – just so long as they did. The atmosphere was buzzing with so much expectation that they believed even the shadow of Peter (one of the apostles) just passing over sick people, would be enough to heal them.

It wasn't only the jammy inhabitants of Jerusalem who hit the jackpot by having these miracle-working guys on their doorstep. Distance was no object and crowds swarmed in from the towns around Jerusalem as well. The Bible says that everyone got healed.

But not everyone was kicking their heels with joy at what was going on.

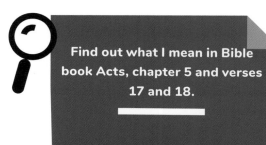

Find out what I mean in Bible book Acts, chapter 5 and verses 17 and 18.

SUPER SERVERS

What do you think of when I say the word 'Christian'?
Do you think of someone who goes to church once a week,
on a Sunday?

Back in the early days of the Church, being a Christian
was an 'all or nothing' sort of thing. As well as being 100%
committed to God, these first Christians allowed the Holy
Spirit into every part of their life, not just on Sundays. For
them it wasn't enough to just *tell* people about Jesus – they
wanted people to have an experience of Him. Whether that
was healing a person in the Holy Spirit's power, or speaking
some encouraging words from God to someone, every day
was a church day.

So when the leaders of this first church found themselves getting bogged down by the day-to-day stuff of leading the church, they figured that it was time to change the way they did things. Up until that point, the church had a dozen leaders (called apostles) who, with the exception of one, were Jesus' disciples when He was on earth. The church they led provided food for those in need, but a dispute had arisen among them about some widows who were getting overlooked in the daily distribution of food.

Something had to be done, but the apostles were keen not to get caught up spending their time serving out food when they should be preaching about Jesus. They hit upon the idea of asking the church to pick seven men to take on the task of giving out the food.

You might think that a mundane job such as that wouldn't require anything particularly spiritual of the people chosen, but think again. As I said, this church made sure that the Holy Spirit was involved in absolutely everything, including something as practical as dishing out food.

You can read about what special qualifications these men needed in Bible book Acts, chapter 6 and verses 3 to 6.

STONED DEAD

Being a Christian way back in the dim and distant past when the Church was just kicking off was mega exciting, but it was also pretty risky. Not everyone liked what the Church was doing, particularly some of the Jewish religious leaders. They'd never been fans of Jesus when He'd been on the scene and they weren't any keener now on these followers of His who seemed to be converting people from their religion in droves. Something had to be done about them... and fast!

One of the Christians (a guy called Stephen) had really rubbed some of these religious people up the wrong way. Stephen was a leader in the Church and was doing great things for God. There seemed to be no stopping this lively leader and when they tried to come against him with a war of words, Stephen's wisdom won the argument hands down.

If they couldn't beat this annoying fella fair and square in their religious debates then there was only one thing for it. They'd have to frame him. Stephen was accused by some lying witnesses of speaking against God (which was a crime in Jewish law) and put on trial. Was Stephen bothered? Not on your life. The Bible tells us that his face was like the face of an angel. Stephen put his confidence in God and wasn't going to be intimidated by any religious lynch mob. He laid into his accusers with a history lesson about God and tried to show them that Jesus was the one their religion had been paving the way for.

Were they having any of it? No way! They didn't want a lecture from this follower of Jesus about how they'd got it wrong. Who did he think he was? When Stephen told them that they were just a bunch of stiff-necked people who got in God's way, they were seething mad.

Did Stephen get let off with a warning for being so blunt? The answer is found in Bible book Acts, chapter 7 and verses 54 through to 60.

PESKY PERSECUTION

While Jesus was alive, He was often met with a mixed reception. Some people loved Him but others (often as not, the Jewish religious leaders) hated Him.

One of the reasons the religious leaders weren't a fan of Jesus was because He criticised them for twisting God's Laws (which were meant to make life better for people) and making them into rules and regulations, which sucked the joy out of life for everyone. Another reason was that Jesus' popularity took people's attention away from the religious leaders. They liked to think that they were the bee's knees and that people should look up to them.

After Jesus' death, His followers became the target for the hatred of the religious leaders. They'd hoped that with Jesus out of the way; they'd be able to get back to their old ways, but not so.

Jesus' followers carried on where He'd left off by telling people that God loved them, and that Jesus had now made it possible for them to know God personally. They also backed up their words by healing the sick, just like Jesus had done. The religious leaders decided to take action and had Stephen (one of Jesus' followers) brought before their Jewish council (the Sanhedrin) and falsely accused of speaking against God, which carried the death sentence.

While the religious leaders did their dirty deed, a young Jew called Saul, looked after their cloaks.

Saul became one of the ringleaders in stirring up a great persecution against Jesus' followers. He went from house to house and dragged off men and women alike and had them flung into prison.

Check out one more thing nasty Saul got up to in Bible book Acts, chapter 9 and verse 2.

ROAD RUNNER

Here's a different kind of Bible story to get your teeth into. It kicks off with a follower of Jesus called Philip who was going great guns for God in a place called Samaria. Miracles were happening all over the place and it looked like he'd be there for ages because God was using him so powerfully.

Not so! An angel showed up and told Philip to pack his bags and to head off in a certain direction, which he dutifully did. Faithful Phil hot-footed it to the old road that ran from Jerusalem to Gaza. Just as he arrived, a posh carriage came into view. Inside sat one of the Queen of Ethiopia's main men, on his way back from worshipping God in Jerusalem.

Time for our Phil's next instruction. The Holy Spirit told him to hurry over to the carriage and stick close to it. As Philip jogged alongside it, he could hear its occupant reading from the book of the prophet Isaiah. Hey, this looked promising.

Philip asked the Ethiopian if he had any idea what the stuff he was reading meant. The guy hadn't a clue so Phil filled him in. He climbed on board, took a seat and launched into telling the VIP next to him that the Bible bit was all about Jesus and how Jesus had died to take the punishment for all the things people do wrong and how anyone can get to know God because of Jesus.

The Ethiopian wanted to become a follower of Jesus. He jumped down from the carriage and got Philip to baptise him in a river by the roadside.

Now for the supernatural bit, but you're going to have to look this up for yourself in Bible book Acts, chapter 8 and verses 38 through to 40. You'll be amazed!

FROM SAUL
TO PAUL

This is a bit confusing but there was a guy called Paul who used to be called Saul. When he was Saul, he was a big-time Bible baddy. Boo! Hiss! He got his kicks from hating anybody who followed Jesus and he spent all his spare time making their life an absolute misery. He'd been involved in the murder of Stephen (who'd been stoned to death) and he'd tried his level best to completely wipe out the Church, going from house to house, dragging out believers in Jesus and flinging them into jail. Saul (later Paul) was the original Mr Nasty, but all of that was about to change.

He was on his way to Damascus to do more dastardly deeds when he was stopped in his tracks by a bright light that flashed around him. As he collapsed on the ground in a heap, a voice called out to him. It was none other than Jesus Himself. He wanted to know why Saul was giving Him such a hard time, but Saul didn't have an answer.

Saul had mistakenly thought that by going after follows of Jesus, he'd been serving the purposes of God. He now realised how wrong he'd been. Jesus told Saul to finish his journey to Damascus where He'd tell him what to do next.

When Saul opened his eyes he couldn't see a thing. He was as blind as a bat and had to be led the rest of the way by his travelling companions. He didn't eat or drink a thing for the next three days until a man called Ananias showed up and said that God had sent him with a message for Saul.

To cut a long story short, he was going to have to change almost everything about his life – including his name from Saul to Paul!

If you want to discover what the message was, then head for Bible book Acts, chapter 9 and read verses 17 to 19.

FOOD FOR THOUGHT

If you'd lived in Israel a couple of thousand years ago, you'd have had to put up with the Romans running the show. They weren't all bad, and some of them even bought into the Jewish religion. One of them, a Roman army captain called Cornelius, worshipped God and helped the Jewish poor people. God appeared to this kind man in a vision and told him to send some men to fetch a guy called Simon Peter who was staying in the seaside town of Joppa. Cornelius dispatched three of his men to go get him, and as they drew near to Joppa, Simon Peter went and had a vision of his own.

He was up on the roof praying when he got a bit peckish. While his food was being prepared for him, God served up a weird vision of a large sheet being lowered down from heaven, which was choc-a-block full of all kinds of animals that Jewish people were forbidden by their law to eat. God then shocked Simon Peter by telling him to kill the animals and to eat them. Peter refused point blank, but God wasn't going to be put off that easily. God repeated the vision. In fact, He showed it to Peter three times in all just to make sure he got the message.

At that moment, Cornelius' men arrived and Simon Peter agreed to return with them to see their master. The Jewish religion forbade Jews from visiting non-Jews (called Gentiles) but Peter now realised that God had given him the vision to show that this was to change. God wanted all people to worship Him, whoever they were and wherever they came from.

Want to discover how this story ends? Then head in the direction of Bible book Acts, chapter 10 and look up verses 47 and 48.

DOUBLE TROUBLE

The Bible features a few people who changed their names, including a chap called Saul who, on becoming a follower of Jesus, began to be known as Paul. From then on, Paul spent much of his life travelling here, there and everywhere telling people about Jesus.

He was joined on one of his epic adventures by Barnabas as they visited various places around the Mediterranean region. The plan was to make a beeline for the Jewish synagogues in these towns and cities so that they could explain to their fellow Jews that Jesus was the Christ (or Messiah) their nation had been waiting for.

For your information, the Christ was a person God had promised the Jewish people to save them. Many of the Jews mistakenly imagined that this Christ would rescue them from their Roman rulers but God's plan was that Jesus would save people from their sinful lives.

So, when Paul and Barnabas started to give this message in the synagogues it didn't always go down too well and they were seen as troublemakers.

To be fair, some of the Jews wanted to find out more and kept an open mind. But although Paul was at pains to explain to them, using their Jewish scriptures, that what they were saying was true, others gave them a frosty reception.

When Paul pointed out that Jesus was God's Saviour for the Gentiles (non-Jews) as well it didn't help matters. Many of the religious leaders were of the opinion that they had the monopoly on God.

They also didn't like it when Paul taught that the Gentiles didn't need to follow any of their Jewish customs or laws to get right with God. All they had to do was to put their faith in Jesus.

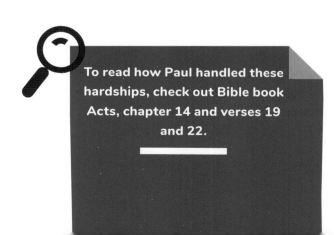

To read how Paul handled these hardships, check out Bible book Acts, chapter 14 and verses 19 and 22.

THAT SETTLES IT!

You've already been introduced to Paul and Barnabas in this book and this time we meet them in a place called Antioch. The followers of Jesus there were being taught, by some Jewish believers, that they needed to comply with Jewish customs and laws to be a true believer.

Paul and Barnabas strongly disagreed with their take on things and decided to settle this once and for all by seeking the advice of the apostles and elders (the top church leaders) in Jerusalem.

Because more and more non-Jewish (Gentile) people were becoming followers of Jesus, it was important to resolve this matter, once and for all.

One of the apostles, Peter (you may remember him as one of Jesus' disciples) piped up and reminded them of a vision God had given him a while back, which made crystal clear that there was no longer to be any distinction between Jews and Gentiles. Faith in Jesus was the only thing anyone needed to become friends with God.

It was then the turn of the dynamic duo of Paul and Barnabas to tell everyone about some of the miracles and amazing things God had been doing among the Gentiles. If God wasn't putting any stumbling blocks in the way of the Gentile believers, who were they to make things difficult.

The church leaders drafted a letter to the church in Antioch, Syria and Cilicia explaining their decision.

The apostles and elders chose a couple of their own men (Judas and Silas) to return with Paul and Barnabas to deliver the letter by hand.

**Want to read what they wrote?
Look up Bible book Acts,
chapter 15 and verses 23 to 29.**

THATAWAY

One person who crops up a lot in the Bible is a guy called Paul. Not only is he famous for writing some sizeable chunks of the New Testament, he's also renowned for his epic journeys around the Mediterranean region.

It wasn't the case that Paul had the travel bug and couldn't stay in one place for long. The reason Paul hot-footed it everywhere was to tell people about Jesus. Paul was almost unstoppable in wanting to share his story of how Jesus had changed him from being an enemy of the Christian Church to its number one fan.

Over his lifetime Paul made three mahoosive journeys across land and sea, which took him around 16 years in total. As he travelled, Paul shared his faith, but also encouraged other Christians and helped start new churches. But it was certainly not all plain sailing! Paul got shipwrecked as well as attacked, beaten and imprisoned.

For now, we're going to focus on Paul's second journey, which took him from Israel, around the north of the Mediterranean, all the way to Greece and back again to where he'd started. That hadn't always been the plan. Paul's intention was to go into Asia, but I'll tell you about that in a moment.

About a quarter of the way along his trip, at a place called Lystra, Paul was joined by a young fella called Timothy, who became his travelling companion and right-hand man on his travels. Now, if you've ever seen a sat nav in a car, you'll probably know that some of them can redirect you to a faster route when you're about to hit bad traffic. Paul and Timothy didn't have anything like that in those days, but what they did have was the Holy Spirit. As the dynamic duo prepared to enter into Asia, the Holy Spirit redirected them towards where He wanted them to go.

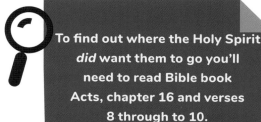

To find out where the Holy Spirit *did* want them to go you'll need to read Bible book Acts, chapter 16 and verses 8 through to 10.

SEETHING SILVERMSITHS

On his third amazing jouney, Paul settled in the city of Ephesus and put all his efforts into trying to persuade its citizens that Jesus was the Son of God, building up the new community of Jesus followers. Wherever Paul went, he healed the sick and performed mighty miracles in God's power. Over time hordes of Ephesians became believers in Jesus and quit worshipping their man-made gods. Not everyone saw this as a good thing.

A chap called Demetrius (a silversmith), who made silver shrines of the Ephesian goddess Artemis, was beginning to feel the pinch. Business was going from bad to worse as more and more people gave up worshipping Artemis. Something had to be done, and fast. Demetrius called an emergency meeting of anyone and everyone whose livelihood had taken a nose dive since Paul had hit town.

His fellow workers were hopping mad with Paul's meddling, and very soon the whole city was in uproar. 'Great is Artemis of the Ephesians!' (Acts 19:28) they chanted. Paul was nowhere to be found, so the angry mob grabbed his travelling companions (Gaius and Aristarchus) and frog-marched them to the city's meeting place. Paul wanted to address the crowd but he was persuaded against doing so. He'd be ripped apart in seconds.

For two hours the Ephesians kept up their chanting until they were eventually quietened down by the city clerk. He reminded the inhabitants of Ephesus that if they had a complaint against Paul they should take him to court. His tactics worked and the crowd dispersed.

Did Paul hang around to risk stirring another commotion? Head for Bible book Acts, chapter 20 and verse 1 to find out.

VERY APPEALING

There was probably only one person who narked the Jewish religious leaders more than Jesus and it was that fella called Paul. Paul was actually a follower of Jesus and he'd made it his business to tell the world that Jesus was God's Son who'd come to earth to give everyone a second chance with God. The reason these religious leaders didn't take too kindly to Paul is because they didn't believe that Jesus was the Messiah (a special person sent by God) that the Jews had been waiting for.

Paul had been arrested by the Romans for disrupting the peace after a crowd of angry Jews had nearly lynched him. Next up, he was brought before the Jewish Sanhedrin (a meeting of the Jewish big shots) to explain himself. In no time at all this also turned nasty and, once again, Paul had to be rescued by the Romans before he was torn to shreds.

While Paul was safely under lock and key in a Roman fort, word reached him that a plot had been hatched by a group of angry Jews to kill him. The plan was to get Paul out from the protection of the Romans back to the Sanhedrin court – under the pretence of needing to ask him some more questions – and then to ambush him along the way. But Paul got his nephew to tell the Romans just what monkey business the Jews were planning, and Lysias (the Roman commander) lost no time in doing something to stop it. At dead of night, he rallied 200 of his officers, 70 cavalry and 200 armed soldiers to escort Paul to Caesarea and into the safekeeping of its governor, Felix.

Surprise surprise, five days later the Jewish high priest turned up with some elders and a lawyer (named Tertullus) in tow. They tried to smooth-talk Governor Felix into handing Paul over to them but Felix wasn't stupid. He knew what their game was.

What happened next? Did Paul get released?

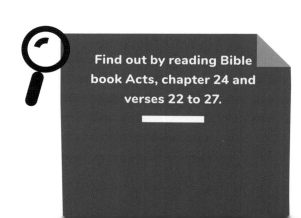

Find out by reading Bible book Acts, chapter 24 and verses 22 to 27.

SHIPWRECK SHAMBLES

Paul was a man on a mission to tell as many people as possible about Jesus. Along the way he'd made a fair few enemies and had ended up getting arrested. Paul protested his innocence and as a Roman citizen demanded a fair trial, which is why he was on his way to Rome.

Paul and his fellow prisoners were sailing with an armed escort across the Mediterranean Sea but the weather had taken a turn for the worse. Winter was fast approaching and the ship was sheltering on the Greek island of Crete, but the harbour was no good for spending the winter. The decision was made to sail round the island to somewhere a bit more suitable.

Soon after they'd set sail, a hurricane-force gale caught them by surprise and drove the ship out to sea. The storm was so bad the crew had to hold the ship together with ropes just to stop it breaking up into pieces. Things went from bad to worse. The sky was as black as night and the ship's crew feared ever seeing daylight, let alone dry land, ever again.

Just when everyone thought that all hope was lost, Paul had an unexpected visitor. One of God's angels turned up and told Paul that God would protect him and everyone on the ship. All 276 of 'em would survive but the ship was a gonner.

Sure enough, after 14 terrifying days at sea, the sailors discovered that they were not far from the shore and decided to run the ship aground on the beach. Before they reached it, the ship crashed onto a sandbank and started to break up in the pounding waves.

Did Paul and his travelling companions make it ashore like the angel had promised? Read Bible book Acts, chapter 27 and verses 42 through to 44 for an answer.

LOTS OF LETTERS

Are you up for learning a new word? OK, so you may have heard it before but I'm guessing the word 'epistle' is not one most of us use every day, if at all.

If you're wondering what epistle means, it's just a fancy word the Bible uses for a letter, particularly one sent by an apostle (church leader). Since many of the New Testament books were originally written as letters to churches or groups of people, we know them as the epistles.

An epistle would have been written on a scroll (they didn't have email then) and was often dictated before being delivered by a messenger. Some of these letters were written to specific churches or groups but others were written for anyone and everyone. That said, all of the epistles are full of essential things that followers of Jesus need to know.

A whopping 13 of these epistles were written by the apostle Paul, so we're going to take a look at one of them and discover the sort of things he wanted to write about. The first epistle of Paul that we come across in the Bible is called Romans but at the time of writing Paul had never ever set foot in Rome. Paul actually wrote this letter from a place called Corinth in Greece and used it to remind the church in Rome of some of the basics of the Christian faith.

Here's his main point in a nutshell: Everyone deserves condemnation from God because of their rebellion against him, but God's grace has provided forgiveness for our sins (and the chance to be friends with God again) through Jesus.

One particularly passionate apostle was James. He reminded everyone in his epistle that reading 'the Word' (Bible) isn't enough. He says they need to do it! But do what? All the stuff that Jesus had talked about.

James challenges them: 'Suppose a rich man wearing a gold ring and fine clothes comes to your meeting, and a poor man in ragged clothes also comes' (James 2:2).

James is encouraging his readers to treat everyone the same.

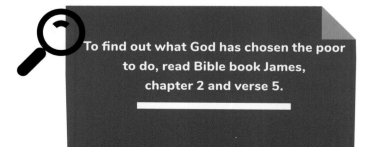

To find out what God has chosen the poor
to do, read Bible book James,
chapter 2 and verse 5.

HAPPY ENDING

When it comes to writing a book, the advice that's often given is to make sure it has a beginning, a middle and an end. Although the Bible is not a story book, it still fits the bill when it comes to this handy writing tip.

The Bible begins with giving us the lowdown on how the world came into being at the very beginning of time. It then tells the story of how the people God had created, turned their backs on Him and how things went from bad to worse as a result. So that's the beginning bit. But the story didn't end there.

The Bible goes on to tell how God set about getting everyone back to being His friends. This is the middle bit. How did God do this? Well, in a nutshell, God launched a brand-new nation (Israel) so that He could remind people that He was still alive and kicking. God then sent Jesus to be born in Israel and to take the punishment for people turning their backs on God. With His mission accomplished, Jesus went back to heaven, but not before He'd trained up a team of people to tell the world that God had forgiven them.

The very last book of the Bible goes by the name of Revelation. This is where we get to read about how it all ends. God's plan was not only to make it possible for everyone to be friends with Him again, but also for us to live in a wonderful, unspoiled world once more. That would mean the whole universe getting a make-over from God.

Is that possible? Time to read about the Bible's happy ending.

Off you go to Bible book Revelation, chapter 21 and verses 1 to 4.